TRUE OR FALSE?

This photo shows a crime scene.

EVIDENCE EVIDENCE EVIDENCE EVIDENCE EVIDENCE EVIDENCE

TRUE!

And it wasn't a hit-and-run! A criminal dropped this tire iron right after a shooting. The crime scene photographer wanted to capture it on film. He didn't get the shot right the first time. So he moved in closer and got more light on the tire iron.

Long after the tire iron is bagged as evidence, the photo will show where it was found. Who knows? It might be the key to solving the case.

Book design Red Herring Design/NYC

Library of Congress Cataloging-in-Publication Data
Webber, Diane, 1968–
Shot and framed : photographers at the crime scene / by Diane Webber.
p. cm. — (24/7: science behind the scenes)
Includes bibliographical references and index.
ISBN-13: 978-0-531-12063-7 (lib. bdg.)   978-0-531-15460-1 (pbk.)
ISBN-10: 0-531-12063-5 (lib. bdg.)   0-531-15460-2 (pbk.)
1. Legal photography—Juvenile literature. 2. Criminal
investigation—Juvenile literature. 3. Evidence, Criminal—Juvenile
literature. 4. Electronic surveillance—Juvenile literature. 5.
Vocational guidance—Juvenile literature. I. Title.
HV6071.W43 2007
363.25'2—dc22   2006025863

SHOT AND FRAMED

Photographers at the Crime Scene

Diane Webber

WARNING: Looking at crime scene photography can be really gruesome. Usually, the images that crime scene photographers capture are scenes that most people would rather not see. View at your own risk.

Franklin Watts®
A Division of Scholastic Inc.
New York • Toronto • London • Auckland • Sydney
Mexico City • New Delhi • Hong Kong
Danbury, Connecticut

CONTENTS

TRUE-LIFE CASE FILES!

These cases are 100% real. Find out how forensic photographers solved some pretty intense mysteries.

Photo from a 50-year-old murder in Cleveland, OH.

15 Case #1:

The Mysterious Murder of Marilyn Sheppard

More than 50 years ago, her murder shocked the nation. Can the crime scene photos show who really did it?

25 Case #2:

The Case of the Too-Tall Robber

Someone goes to jail for stealing $200 from a store. Can photography show if police got the right man?

Can security cameras in Milpitas, CA, help free a man?

Strip malls like this one were being robbed in Cedar Falls, IA.

35 Case #3:

The Hole in the Wall Gang

A group of thieves is robbing store after store. Can crime scene photography put an end to their spree?

5

FORENSIC DOWNLOAD

Now do you get the picture? If not, here are more angles on forensic photography.

YELLOW PAGES

Police try not to disturb a crime scene. But soon everything returns to normal. Bodies get taken to the morgue. Evidence goes to the police station.

FORENSIC 411

So, how do detectives remember what was where? That's a job for a forensic photographer.

IN THIS SECTION:

▶ how forensic photographers REALLY TALK;

▶ how PHOTOGRAPHERS work a crime scene;

▶ and whom they work with when they're ON THE JOB.

Ready, Aim, Shoot!

Crime scene photographers have their own way of talking. Find out what their vocabulary means.

"You don't know anything about crime scene photography. Wait until the pros get here."

crime scene photography
(krime seen fuh-TOG-ruh-fee) taking pictures of evidence after a crime happens

forensic photography
(fuh-REN-sik fuh-TOG-ruh-fee) photography that can be used to solve crimes or settle lawsuits

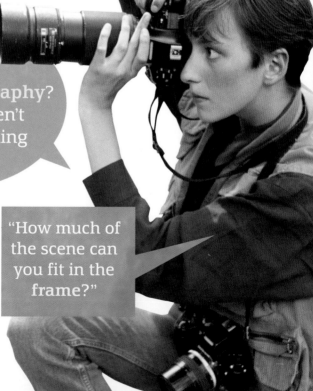

"Are you the expert in forensic photography? Good, we haven't touched anything yet."

"How much of the scene can you fit in the frame?"

frame
(fraym) what you see when you look through the camera or look at the screen to take a photo

> "Let's first get an **overview** shot of the crime scene."

overview
(OH-vur-vyoo) a photograph that shows the entire scene. Overview photos are taken from a distance.

> "Next we want **close-ups** of the body."

close-up
(KLOHSS-uhp) a photograph in which a small detail fills the whole picture. A close-up is the opposite of an overview.

> "What **mid-range** shots do you think we'll need?"

mid-range
(mid-RAYNJ) a photograph that is in between a close-up and an overview

Say What?

Here's other lingo crime scene photographers might use on the job.

photo, pic, shot
(FOH-toh, pik, shot) all refer to a photograph
"We want a **shot** of the body. You know, a **pic**, a **photo**— am I speaking English?!"

photog
(FOH-tog) short for *photographer*
"Well, since I'm a **photog**, I think I get the picture. Get it?"

the 360
(the three-SIKS-tee) an overview that captures all angles of a crime scene
"Let me just take **the 360** one more time. I don't want to miss anything."

mug shots
(muhg shots) *mug* is slang for *face*. Mug shots are taken of anyone charged with a crime.
"Take these **mug shots**. Show them to the witnesses and see if we can get a match."

THE OVERVIEW PHOTOGRAPH: WHERE IT HAPPENED

A hiker is missing. The local police suspect there's been a crime.

The crime scene photographer arrives and takes this overview photo. It shows almost the whole scene. The photographer may take lots of overview shots to show the area from all angles. That's known as "the 360." Overview shots are especially helpful when a case goes to trial. They give **jurors** the feeling that they were actually there.

CRIME SCENE DO NOT ENTER

footprint

the details in context

glove

THE MID-RANGE PHOTOGRAPH: THE EVIDENCE

The police have spotted a backpack, a water bottle, and a muddy glove.

Now it's time to focus in on the **evidence**. The photographer takes mid-range shots. She shoots the evidence in context. That means that she is careful to show exactly where each piece of evidence was found.

THE CLOSE-UP PHOTOGRAPH: THE EVIDENCE IN DETAIL

The photographer spots a footprint.

Finally, the photographer focuses on smaller things— like a footprint. She often photographs the evidence next to a measuring tape or a ruler. Close-ups are usually blown up big for juries to see. The ruler shows the actual size of the evidence.

individual details

Shot and Framed

Overview. Mid-range. Close-up. Crime scene photographers don't just get the big picture. They also focus on the details.

Most crime scenes buzz with activity. Detectives try to piece together what happened. **Experts** dust for fingerprints. If someone's been killed, a medical examiner examines the body. But they all work with one rule in mind: Don't disturb anything until the crime scene photographer does her work.

Photographing a crime scene is tougher than it sounds. First the photographer does a **walkthrough**. She tours the crime scene, talking to detectives about what happened and what needs to be photographed.

Next come the photos. She takes three kinds of photos: overviews, mid-range shots, and close-ups. Like the other **investigators**, she has to be careful not to disturb the evidence.

Then it's back to the lab to **process** the pictures— and possibly take more. Fingerprints, for instance, might be invisible until they're treated with chemicals in a lab. Then they get photographed, too.

In the end, every crime scene is preserved in hundreds of photos. Detectives use them to recall the scene. Lawyers use them to show juries what happened. Sometimes all it takes is one to put a criminal in jail.

The Forensic Team

Forensic photographers work as part of a team to help solve crimes.

POLICE OFFICERS

Officers are the first to arrive at a crime scene. They make sure everyone is safe. They keep the public away. Then they help gather evidence.

CRIME SCENE PHOTOGRAPHERS

They take pictures at crime scenes. Their images help investigators solve cases. They can also serve as evidence in court.

DETECTIVES

These are the officers who lead investigations. At a crime scene, they often point out what needs to be photographed.

EVIDENCE CUSTODIANS

They collect evidence after it is photographed. They keep notes and store evidence at the police lab.

PROSECUTORS

They are lawyers who bring suspects to trial. They often use crime scene photographs in trials.

LAB TECHNICIANS

They process and analyze crime scene photos.

TRUE-LIFE CASE FILES!

24 hours a day, 7 days a week, 365 days a year, forensic photographers are helping to solve mysteries.

IN THIS SECTION:

▶ how an FBI agent used 50-year-old photos to solve a FAMOUS MURDER CASE;

▶ whether a BLURRY VIDEOTAPE can help identify a masked thief;

▶ if police can make a BURGLAR'S FINGERPRINT appear out of nowhere.

Here's how investigators work with forensic crime scene photographers.

What does it take to solve a crime? Good criminal investigators don't just make guesses. They're like scientists. They follow a step-by-step process.

As you read the case studies, you can follow along with them. Keep an eye out for the icons below. They'll clue you in to each step along the way.

THE QUESTION

At the beginning of a case, investigators settle on **one or two main questions** they have to answer.

THE EVIDENCE

The next step is to **gather and analyze evidence**—including photos. Investigators gather as much information as they can. Then they study it and figure out what it means.

THE CONCLUSION

Along the way, investigators come up with theories to explain what happened. They test their theories against crime scene photos and other evidence. Does the evidence back up the theory? **If so, they've reached a conclusion.** And chances are they've cracked the case.

The Mysterious Murder of Marilyn Sheppard

More than 50 years ago, her murder shocked the nation. Can the crime scene photos show who really did it?

"They've Killed Marilyn!"

A Cleveland doctor's wife has been murdered. Her husband is the only witness.

In the 1950s, Bay Village, Ohio, was a peaceful place. This wealthy suburb of Cleveland had a low crime rate. Murder was rarely in the news—until July 4, 1954.

Early that morning, a call came in to the police station. It was from the mayor of Bay View, Spencer Houk. His neighbor Marilyn Sheppard had been killed!

Police arrived at the scene at 6:02 A.M. It was clear Ms. Sheppard was dead. The 31-year-old woman lay in bed. She was covered in blood. Her husband, Dr. Sam Sheppard, said the killer had escaped.

Photographers took pictures all around the house. They found signs of robbery. Someone had searched through the desk downstairs. Dr. Sheppard's medical bag lay open on the lawn. Some medicine was missing. But there were no signs of a break-in.

Marilyn Sheppard was found dead in her house on July 4, 1954. Her husband said he tried to catch the killer, but the man escaped.

Dr. Sheppard told his story to police. That night, he had fallen asleep on the couch. He woke up when he heard his wife yelling for him. He ran into a "bushy-haired man" in the hallway. They fought, and the man knocked Dr. Sheppard out.

When Dr. Sheppard woke up, he chased the man outside. Their second fight ended the same way, with Sheppard knocked out on the ground.

Dr. Sam Sheppard and Marilyn Sheppard water-skiing in the early days of their marriage.

Bay Village, Ohio, is located right on Lake Erie. In the 1950s, it was a quiet suburb of Cleveland. Nothing much happened there. But then, on the morning of July 4, 1954, a doctor shocked the town with some news. His wife had been killed.

When Dr. Sheppard came to, he went back inside. Marilyn Sheppard was dead. The couple's seven-year-old son, Sam, was still asleep.

That's when Sheppard called Houk. "For God's sake, Spen, get over here," he cried. "I think they've killed Marilyn!"

The crime shocked the nation. But did it really happen the way Sheppard said it did?

On Trial

Did the doctor kill his own wife?

A police officer discovered a stained T-shirt in Lake Erie, near the Sheppards' home. It may have been Dr. Sheppard's missing shirt.

In a week, the story was all over the newspapers. Soon there was one question on everyone's mind. Was Dr. Sheppard telling the truth?

Pieces of Dr. Sheppard's story didn't seem to make sense. Ms. Sheppard had been killed between 3 and 3:30 A.M. Her watch stopped at 3:15 A.M. But it was almost 6 A.M. when Dr. Sheppard called Houk. Had he really been knocked out on the beach all that time?

Also, Dr. Sheppard had been wearing a T-shirt during dinner that evening. By morning it had disappeared. He couldn't tell police where

During Dr. Sheppard's trial, the jury visited the crime scene. Here, they're walking up from the beach behind the Sheppard's home. Dr. Sheppard is in the middle of the staircase.

it was. He also said he had checked his wife's pulse twice. But he had none of her blood on him. Police asked if he had washed up. He said no.

To police, the case didn't seem like a robbery. The **coroner** said the killer was in a rage. Ms. Sheppard had been stabbed 35 times. Why would a robber be so angry at her?

Detectives looked deeper into the Sheppards' private lives. Their marriage was not as happy as it looked. Police asked Dr. Sheppard to take a lie-detector test. He refused.

Eventually, **prosecutors** had enough evidence. They charged Dr. Sheppard with murder. In December 1954, a jury found him guilty. He was sent to prison for life.

But the case was far from over. Sheppard **appealed** the decision. His lawyers claimed he didn't get a fair trial. The jurors must have been too influenced by news reports, they said. The trial should have been moved far away from Bay Village.

The appeal took ten years. Finally, a judge agreed with Dr. Sheppard's lawyers. Sheppard got a new trial. He was found not guilty.

Dr. Sam Sheppard was free. But he had problems with drugs and alcohol. Four years after he left prison, he died.

Dr. Sheppard's story, however, did not die. It led to a TV show and a movie called *The Fugitive*. Several authors wrote books about the murder. Some thought Dr. Sheppard killed his wife. Others insisted he was innocent.

One of those people was Sam Reese Sheppard. Sam was just seven when his mother was killed. He wanted to prove that his father was innocent.

Sam Reese Sheppard argued that his father was innocent of his mother's murder. Here, he speaks outside the U.S. Supreme Court building on September 18, 1999.

A BIG DECISION
Trials of famous cases are now often moved.

The U.S. Supreme Court is the highest court in the country. In 1966, the Supreme Court got involved in this case. It ruled that Dr. Sam Sheppard didn't get a fair trial. The court said that newspaper coverage made the jury **biased**.

The decision changed the way famous cases are handled. Today, trials of famous cases are often moved to different towns.

Picturing the Crime

An FBI agent looks back at the evidence.

In 1999, Sam Reese Sheppard sued the City of Cleveland. He wanted prosecutors to admit they had made a mistake.

The city had to prepare a defense. They called in a crime scene expert, Gregg McCrary.

McCrary had a huge job. The records from the two trials totaled about 7,500 pages. "My role was . . . to put the pieces of the puzzle together," McCrary told Crime Library.com. "I was there to show what was more likely to have occurred than not."

The most interesting evidence McCrary had were photos—all 1,600 of them.

Retired FBI agent Gregg McCrary was called in to examine the records from Dr. Sheppard's first trial. In addition to the written records McCrary studied, he also reviewed 1,600 photographs.

McCrary had one basic question to answer. Did the photos tell the same story as Sheppard's?

THE QUESTION

McCrary studied the pictures. He knew there were three main crime scenes. The body was found in the bedroom. The hallway was where Sheppard and the attacker first fought. And the beach was where the second fight took place. Each site might hold important clues.

THE EVIDENCE

This crime scene photo shows Dr. Sheppard's jacket on a couch downstairs in their home. Dr. Sheppard claimed that the night of his wife's murder, he had fallen asleep on this couch.

21

Set Up

The photos make it look like a burglary. Or do they?

This photo shows evidence found at the crime scene. Marilyn Sheppard's watch *(circled)* has been placed in a bottle. The watch was found downstairs in the Sheppard's home. There was blood on it.

To McCrary, the photos showed one thing clearly. The scene had been **staged**. In other words, the killer set up the scene to fool police. He made it look like murder wasn't his main goal. The scene had been set up to look like a drug-related burglary.

What made McCrary think this wasn't a burglary? First of all, he noticed the extreme violence of the murder. The killer had lost control. And yet, the house was in pretty good shape. A few desk drawers had been pulled out. Some trophies were broken. The state of the house didn't fit the extreme violence of the murder.

McCrary decided that the crime scene was staged—badly. The burglary was just a cover story. And his real **motive** was simple: to kill Marilyn Sheppard.

Spattered or Smeared?

Bloodstains tell a story that's not the same as Sheppard's.

Next, McCrary looked for bloodstains in the photos. Dr. Sheppard said he had touched his wife's body. He had stroked her face. Sheppard

claimed he did not wash up before police arrived.

If these things were true, where was the blood? Sheppard had only a small bloodstain on his knee. The phone he used to call the Houks was clean. Photos of his watch showed more blood. But it was spattered, not smeared. During an attack, blood tends to spatter. Was the watch near Ms. Sheppard when she was attacked?

Dr. Sheppard on July 30, 1954. He had just been charged with his wife's murder. On his neck is a collar from an injury he said was caused by his wife's killer.

The killer, too, would have been covered in Ms. Sheppard's blood. Where was it? Dr. Sheppard had wrestled with the killer twice. But he only had that one bloodstain.

Dr. Sheppard also claimed the killer went through his pockets while he was knocked out. The man supposedly stole Sheppard's watch, keys, ring, and wallet. Police found the stolen goods outside the house. Yet there was very little blood on any of the items. They found none around Sheppard's pocket.

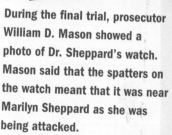

McCrary tried to match Sheppard's story to the crime scene photos. The pieces didn't fit. "Blood *was not* where it should have been," McCrary told CrimeLibrary.com, "and it *was* where it should not have been."

During the final trial, prosecutor William D. Mason showed a photo of Dr. Sheppard's watch. Mason said that the spatters on the watch meant that it was near Marilyn Sheppard as she was being attacked.

Final Decision?

McCrary testifies, and the jury listens.

FULLY UPDATED REVISION OF THE CLASSIC BEST-SELLER

CRIME CLASSIFICATION MANUAL

SECOND EDITION

A STANDARD SYSTEM FOR INVESTIGATING AND CLASSIFYING VIOLENT CRIMES

JOHN E. DOUGLAS, ANN W. BURGESS, ALLEN G. BURGESS, and ROBERT K. RESSLER

This book divides crimes into categories. Crimes that fit a certain pattern are placed in the same category.

THE CONCLUSION

McCrary was ready to make his final report. But first he checked a book called the *Crime Classification Manual*. According to that book, the Sheppard case fit the pattern for a "staged domestic homicide." That's when one family member kills another. These crimes usually involve a lot of violence. Strange things are taken from the scene. The killer leaves no murder weapon or fingerprints. Each of these things described the Sheppard case perfectly.

McCrary closed his investigation. The photos and other evidence pointed to one conclusion. Sam Sheppard killed his wife.

In the spring of 2000, McCrary spoke in court. The jury agreed with McCrary and other witnesses for the defense. They refused to declare Dr. Sheppard innocent.

Sam Reese Sheppard lost his case. But his belief in his father's innocence remains as strong as ever.

"My father's life was destroyed by the state of Ohio," Sam told reporters. "I will never forget that. I will never let you forget that." 24/7

For McCrary, photographic evidence pointed to Sam Sheppard's guilt. Can photo evidence be used to prove someone is innocent? Read the next case to find out.

Milpitas, California
October 1998–June 2006

The Case of the Too-Tall Robber

Someone goes to jail for stealing $200 from a store. Can high-tech photography show if police got the right man?

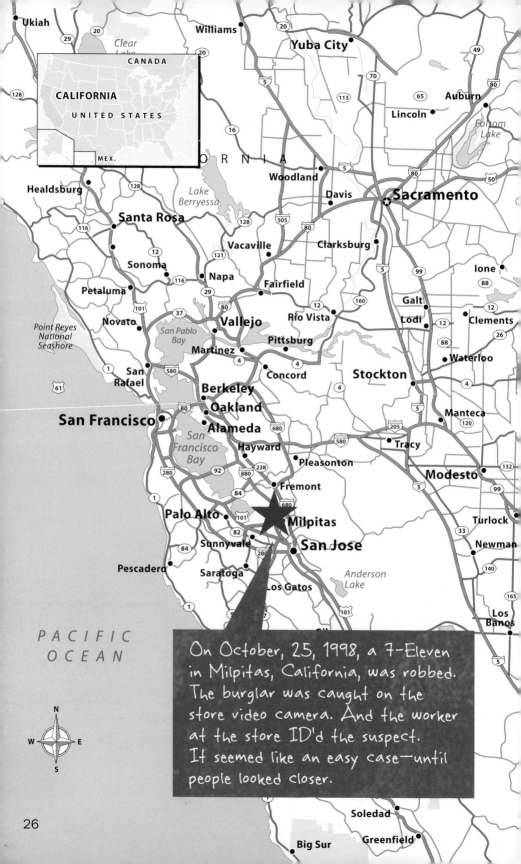

On October, 25, 1998, a 7-Eleven in Milpitas, California, was robbed. The burglar was caught on the store video camera. And the worker at the store ID'd the suspect. It seemed like an easy case—until people looked closer.

A Masked Man

Video and an eyewitness both "see" the same thing. The police have their man. Or do they?

On October 25, 1998, police in Milpitas, California, got a call. A masked man had burst into the 7-Eleven store on Milpitas Boulevard. He wore a stocking over his head. He jumped over the counter. He took $200 from the cash register. Then he ran out the door. He was in and out of the store in less than two minutes.

At the scene, the case looked simple. A security camera had videotaped the entire robbery. A store clerk witnessed it as well. Everyone thought they knew the thief.

The investigating officer talked to the store manager, Richard Scott Salet. The two men looked at the security video. The burglar looked like a man named Michael Hutchinson. Both the officer and Salet had known Hutchinson since they were children.

A man with a stocking over his head (like this man) robbed a 7-Eleven in Milpitas, CA. Although the man's face wasn't clear, the store manager thought he recognized the thief.

It seemed like a sad story. Hutchinson had been in trouble before. He had served time in jail. But when he left prison, he started a new life. He became pastor of a church. He helped young people. His church even advertised in the 7-Eleven. On the ad was a picture of Hutchinson.

A jury like this one heard Hutchinson's case. Hutchinson's jury found him guilty of the 7-Eleven robbery.

Had the pastor really gone back to a life of crime? There was a lot of evidence against him. The clerk had seen him outside the store before the robbery. Police showed her six mug shots, including Hutchinson's. She picked Hutchinson as the robber.

Police felt they had a case. They arrested Hutchinson. A few months later a jury found him guilty. He was sent to prison for 13 years.

Case closed? It seemed that way. But could it be that an **eyewitness** and a videotape were both wrong?

Questioning the Verdict

Hutchinson fights for his freedom. Will the lawyers and judges help him?

From the moment he was arrested, Hutchinson said he didn't do it. The burglar's face had been covered by a stocking. How could anyone be sure it was him?

At the first trial, Hutchinson's lawyer was Dennis Kazubowski. Kazubowski decided not to **analyze** the security video. Hutchinson spoke in his own defense. He said he was nowhere near the 7-Eleven that day. But he didn't convince the jury.

CRIME SCENE VIDEOGRAPHY

What can convince a jury even more than a photograph? Video.

All over the country, more and more police departments are using crime scene videography on major cases.

Videos have some real advantages over photos, says Wadi Sawabini. He's a crime scene videography instructor. "Say you have a person who has been thrown from a car," Sawabini says. "A video can give you a much better idea of the distance than a photo." The whole jury can also see a video at the same time. Pictures have to be passed from person to person.

But video will never replace still photographs completely at crime scenes. "You need both," says Sawabini. You can't catch a fingerprint on video. For that you need old-fashioned pictures.

Hutchinson decided to appeal the decision. He didn't have much money. So the court named a lawyer to take his case for free. Hutchinson's new lawyer was Robert Gehring. Gehring took a close look at the videotape. He thought the robber looked too short to be Michael Hutchinson.

Gehring wanted the video analyzed with a process called **photogrammetry**. Experts in photogrammetry compare people to other items in a video or a picture. The results can show how tall a **suspect** is.

Gehring asked the court to pay for the photogrammetry. The judges refused. So Gehring did it himself. He and his wife went to the 7-Eleven. They measured shelves, the counter, and other things seen in the video.

A guard keeps an eye on the security videos. In the Hutchinson case, experts argued that the security video proved that he was not the thief.

In 2001, Gehring took his new evidence to court. He showed the video to the judges. He explained his measurements. He had the judges compare the burglar's height to the things he had measured. Surely they would see what Gehring saw. The man was too short to be Hutchinson.

But the court said Gehring's process was not scientific enough. The judges decided that Hutchinson's first trial had been fair. And the pastor stayed in jail.

In the Public Eye

Hutchinson gets help from a newspaper.

Fredric Tulsky is a reporter from the *San Jose Mercury News*. He is one of the reporters who investigated criminal trials in the area.

Five years went by. Finally, Hutchinson got help from a newspaper called the *San Jose Mercury News*. The *Mercury News* covers Milpitas and other towns nearby.

In 2002, editors at the *Mercury News* had their eyes on the courts. They felt that several local trials had ended in unfair rulings.

Reporters started analyzing criminal cases. A reporter named Fredric Tulsky led the investigation. He found that the system sometimes failed. Prosecutors made mistakes. Defense lawyers made mistakes. And the appeals court sometimes ignored those mistakes. "Too many things go wrong in our county's courtrooms," wrote Tulsky's editor, Susan Goldberg. "Too many trials are less fair than they should be. Too little is done to correct these problems, even though many officials are aware of them."

When the legal system makes a mistake, someone is treated unfairly. Sometimes an innocent person goes to jail. Tulsky thought Hutchinson was one of those people. To prove his theory, he went to the videotape.

Let's Go to the Videotape

What can forensic photogrammetry tell us about the robber?

The *Mercury News* now did what Hutchinson's second lawyer had wanted to do. They hired an expert in photogrammetry. His name is Gregg Stutchman.

Stutchman had two questions to answer. How tall is Michael Hutchinson? And how tall is the suspect in the security video?

The first question was easy. Trial records said Hutchinson is 6′1″ or 6′2″ (185–188 cm).

 Gregg Stutchman is an expert in photogrammetry. He can compare a person to other items in a video or picture. The results can determine how tall that person is.

To answer the second question, Stutchman had to go back to the 7-Eleven.

Stutchman brought a camera to the store. He photographed the doorway, the counter, and the cash register. He shot each object from different angles. He also took measurements of all the things he photographed.

Then Stutchman went back to his lab. He used special computer and video equipment to analyze the video. He focused on pictures of the masked burglar. Then he entered the measurements of objects in the store into a computer program. The program used the height of the objects to figure out the height of the burglar.

THE CONCLUSION Stutchman's conclusion didn't surprise Tulsky. The robber stood between 5´2˝ and 5´6˝ (157–168 cm)! Hutchinson, it seemed, was at least six inches (15 cm) taller than the masked man. Hutchinson couldn't be the burglar!

In March 2006, the *Mercury News* published Tulsky's story on Hutchinson. Tulsky printed Stutchman's findings. He pointed out that eyewitnesses can be wrong. In this case, their mistake may have cost a man several years in jail.

Another Chance

The too-tall burglar gets a new trial. Will he go free?

In May 2006, Hutchinson's case went to court again. A judge looked at the evidence. Stutchman spoke. Hutchinson's first lawyer, Dennis Kazubowski, also spoke. He said that he had seen no need to have the tape analyzed. He had thought it was Hutchinson on the videotape, too.

On June 22, 2006, the judge decided the case. Kazubowski had made a mistake, he said. He should have had the video analyzed. The judge gave the state of California 60 days to make a decision. In August 2006, Hutchinson was finally released from jail.

Hutchinson's new lawyer, Lawrence Gibbs, thinks justice is finally being done. "This should have happened six years ago." Gibbs said. "Michael Hutchinson spent six years in prison because the court would not give a couple thousand dollars to his attorney." 24/7

Gregg Stutchman is an expert in forensic photography and in forensic audio. He lives in Napa, CA.

Gregg Stutchman talks about forensic photography.

24/7: How did you get started?

STUTCHMAN: I'm an ex-cop. That's where I learned about forensic photography, on the beat.

24/7: Tell me about your work.

STUTCHMAN: I help people make sense of lousy evidence. We have special equipment that makes video and audio evidence easier to understand. Nothing is as powerful as what can be seen and heard in recorded evidence.

24/7: Tell me about a recent case.

STUTCHMAN: Someone was murdered at the top of a mountain. I had to show that two suspects had time to get from the bottom of the mountain to the top. There was a road, but it couldn't be seen from the sky. The woods were too thick.

We needed pictures to show the jury. So we went down with balloons. We floated them up to the tops of the trees along the road. Then we took 500 photographs from the air. What we had was like a connect-the-dots map. It showed the jury clearly that the suspects had the time to get up the mountain. It was a lot of fun.

In this case, scientific analysis may have freed an innocent man. Can a little scientific work put a slippery gang of thieves in jail? Read the next case to find out.

Black Hawk County, Iowa
1995

The Hole in the Wall Gang

A group of thieves is robbing store after store. Can crime scene photography put an end to their spree?

Holes in the Wall

Police in Iowa are scratching their heads over robberies in a strip mall.

In 1995, a gang of burglars were running wild in Iowa. These thieves were smart. They had a system. They struck strip malls all around Black Hawk County. Each time, they made off with thousands of dollars in cash and goods. And they left almost no clues behind.

The gang worked carefully. They entered from the back of the strip mall.

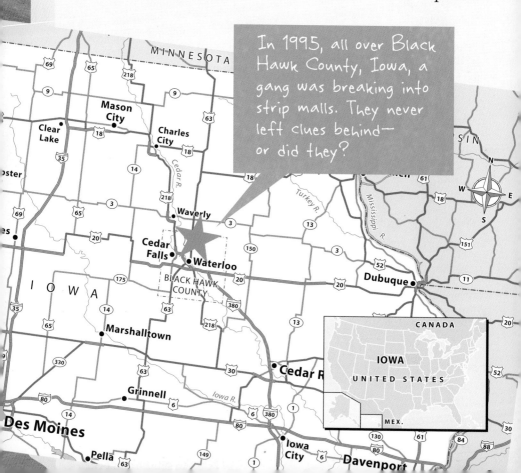

In 1995, all over Black Hawk County, Iowa, a gang was breaking into strip malls. They never left clues behind— or did they?

Burglars in Iowa were robbing strip malls like this one.

They got in by breaking a lock. They looted the first store. Then they got out saws and hammers. They cut a hole in a side wall. And they climbed through to the next store. They took whatever they could. Then they cut another hole. Store by store, they worked their way through the mall.

Police soon identified the pattern behind the crimes. They knew they had a gang on their hands. The crimes were too complicated for a single thief. And they knew it was the same gang each time. Police even gave the thieves a name: the Hole in the Wall Gang.

Beyond that, they didn't know much. After each burglary, police searched for fingerprints. Not a single one had been found. The investigation stalled—until the gang came to Cedar Falls.

Here's how they did it. They drilled holes in the walls that connected the stores.

A Fresh Look

The gang strikes again, and a new detective is on the trail.

Detective Robert Kramer worked for the Cedar Falls Police Department. His specialty? Crime scene photography. His work would help put the Hole in the Wall Gang behind bars.

Detective Robert Kramer is an expert at processing crime scenes. He's been on the police force in Cedar Falls for 26 years. And he'd always loved photography. His skills with a camera have come in handy at crime scenes. Today he teaches forensic photography at the Iowa Law Enforcement Academy.

When the Hole in the Wall Gang struck again, Kramer was ready. He headed for the crime scene. His job: collect evidence and take pictures. At the strip mall, Kramer got to work. The crooks had entered through a back door. Then they cut into the bike shop, the hair salon, the tanning salon, and several other stores. They raided the cash registers. They took anything that looked valuable.

This time, the gang had gotten sloppy. "There was plenty of evidence," Kramer said. "They left all their tools behind. They left footprints."

Detective Kramer took this photo of a footprint at a crime scene. He placed a ruler next to it so he'd know the exact size of the print.

Still, Kramer had one important question. The answer could crack the case open. Did the burglars leave fingerprints?

Kramer had the stores and the tools dusted for prints. Nothing turned up. Then he had an idea. It came to him in a flash.

A Ray of Light

Could the prints be hidden in a common household tool?

One of the burglars' tools caught Kramer's eye. It was a flashlight. It had already been dusted for prints—but only on the outside. What about the inside?

"I figured they were wearing gloves to do the crime," Kramer told 24/7. "But I'll bet you they weren't wearing gloves when they bought that flashlight. I bet they weren't wearing gloves when they were sitting in a Wal-Mart parking lot putting batteries in it."

Kramer put on a pair of gloves himself. He carefully took the batteries out of the flashlight. He couldn't see prints. But that didn't mean they weren't there.

The human eye can't see every fingerprint. A fingerprint left in something sticky is easy to see. Sometimes police find fingerprints left in blood. But more often, fingerprints are left in body oils like sweat. These are usually invisible to the eye. They are called **latent prints**.

Were there latent prints on the batteries? To answer the question, Kramer needed special tools. He put the batteries in a plastic bag. Then he took them back to his lab.

The Smoking Gun
Can a photograph make fingerprints appear out of nowhere?

Kramer set up his tools in the lab. Then he pulled out the most important item: Super Glue. To find prints on hard surfaces— like batteries—experts use a process called Super Glue fuming. Here's how it works.

First, Kramer got an airtight container. Inside, he put a cup of warm water and a small amount of Super Glue. He added the batteries and heated the container. At 120°F (49°C) a chemical in the Super Glue turns to gas. Those fumes stick to proteins. Sweat or oil from a fingertip contains protein. When the fumes meet the proteins, they turn white.

After 15 minutes, Kramer took the batteries out. He noticed a couple of white spots. Could his idea be right?

The prints still weren't clear enough to use. So Kramer took the next step. He soaked the batteries in a special dye. Like the Super Glue fumes, it sticks to proteins.

After a few minutes, Kramer rinsed the batteries with water. He put them under a special light. Then he photographed the batteries. The light made the dye stand out.

Kramer developed the film. And there it was—the evidence he needed. On the pictures were two white fingerprints.

Would the prints lead police to the Hole in the Wall Gang?

Both of these photos are from Detective Kramer's files.
Top: A detail from one of the flashlight batteries found at the crime scene. Kramer used the fuming technique to make the latent prints visible. The white spots are fingerprints.
Above: Kramer then soaked the batteries in a special dye that sticks to fingerprints.

Closing the Holes

The print leads Kramer straight to the thieves.

Kramer's last task was to match the prints with a suspect. Often, police use a computer database of known criminals' fingerprints. But Kramer didn't have to use the computer. "I had the fingerprint cards of a group of suspects on my desk," he said. The prints on the cards came from people who had been arrested before.

Kramer compared the cards to the prints from the battery. He quickly found the owner of one of the prints. "It took me about ten minutes to find a match," he said.

Cedar Falls police arrested the first suspect quickly. He led them to his partner.

Police arrested the second man. They took his prints on a fingerprint card. One of them was a perfect match with the second print from the battery.

Kramer had enough evidence to send the case to trial. A jury found the two men guilty. They went to jail. There, drilling through the walls would not be easy. 24/7

Fingerprint experts use cards like this one to record fingerprints.

FORENSIC DOWNLOAD

Now do you get the picture? Here are more angles on forensic photography.

IN THIS SECTION:

▶ how pictures freed a slave and helped a home full of ORPHANS;

▶ why forensic photography MAKES HEADLINES;

▶ what FORENSIC PHOTOGRAPHERS have in their tool kit;

▶ whether forensic photography might be in YOUR FUTURE.

43

Key Dates in Crime Scene Photography

How did crime scene photography get started? Hint: The camera had to be invented first!

L.J.M. Daguerre.

1839 Forensic First in France

A Frenchman named Louis Daguerre had just invented one of the first cameras. Then he got a job from an angry wife. She asked Daguerre to take a picture of her husband and his girlfriend. She sued for divorce—and used the picture as evidence. The court ruled in favor of the wife. Those first pictures were called daguerreotypes (da-GARE-oh-types).

1859 Forensic First in U.S.: The Case of the Runaway Slave

Lawyers in the U.S. used photographs in court for the first time. An escaped slave argued that he should not be returned to his master. He had been abused, he said. His lawyers took pictures of his scarred back to prove it. The court ruled in favor of the slave.

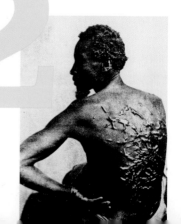

1881 Let's Hear It for the Kids!

Edward Cowley ran an **orphanage** in New York City. He was accused of abusing the kids. Lawyers showed the court "before and after" pictures. When they arrived, children looked healthy. Later, they had been beaten and lost weight. Cowley was **convicted** of "wrongs against children."

1937 Glow-in-the-Dark Blood

Walter Spect had a breakthrough. He was a German forensic scientist. He made a chemical called **luminol**. When it's sprayed on a surface, it makes blood glow. Photographers then take pictures to capture spatter patterns. Luminol can also reveal blood left over after a surface has been cleaned.

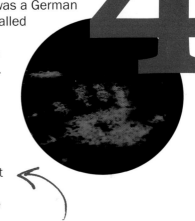

1977 A "Super" New Technique

A Japanese scientist named Masoto Soba developed Super Glue fuming. The process helps make finger-prints **visible** to the eye. The prints can then be photographed.

Go to page 40–41 to learn more about Super Glue fuming.

1978 Video Hits the Big City

Prosecutors in New York City began using video. At first, they recorded confessions by suspects. Later, they videotaped crime scenes. Prosecutors used the tapes to show juries what happened. Today, many police departments use crime scene videography.

2003 Digital Gets a Thumbs-Up

The American Society of Crime Lab Directors approved a **digital** evidence lab in North Carolina. Crime scene photographers had been slow to use digital cameras. They don't want to be accused of changing the images. Today, though, digital photography is becoming more accepted at crime scenes.

Go to pages 50–51 to learn more about the controversy over digital photography.

In the News

Read all about it! Crime scene photography is front-page news.

Actor Gary Dourdan plays Investigator Warrick Brown on *CSI: Crime Scene Investigation*. Because of this show, juries tend to expect clear video evidence, as well as photos of evidence.

Juries Want Cases to Look Like TV!

GREAT FALLS, VIRGINIA—February 2005

The photo above is from the TV show *CSI: Crime Scene Investigation*. But these days, juries on criminal trials expect to see evidence this clear in the courtroom. That's according to Jan Garvin, who works with a group that trains police officers to use video.

Jury members are used to seeing crime scenes on shows like *CSI* and *Forensic Files*. And they want to see them in court, too. "Juries know good video from bad," Garvin says. And in court, they expect to see video as good as what they see on TV.

A police officer writes up a parking ticket. These days, police in Salt Lake City, Utah, are using camera phones to take photos of cars that are illegally parked.

Caught on Film

SALT LAKE CITY—July 6, 2006

This driver should never try this in Salt Lake City, Utah. There, the police are armed with cell phones with digital cameras. They're on the lookout for cars parked in handicap or red no-parking zones. When they find them, they write a ticket and snap a photo.

When the drivers return, they find a ticket—and the photo. Gary Griffiths works for the city. He thinks the photos are important proof of illegal parking. With the photos, "the tickets will be more **valid**," he says.

Capturing lawbreakers on film gives police the proof they need.

Developing the Evidence

Check out the tools and equipment used by a forensic crime scene photographer.

digital camera This is the wave of the future in crime scene photography. Digital cameras allow the photographer to find out immediately if he's gotten a good photo. (See pages 50-51.)

camera Crime scene photographers still have cameras that use film.

filters Sometimes photographers shoot through colored squares of plastic. This can make some evidence show up more clearly. A green tint, for instance, makes blood look black in a photo.

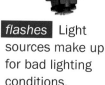

flashes Light sources make up for bad lighting conditions.

lenses A normal (50 mm) lens works for mid-range shots. A **wide-angle** (28 mm) lens gives more of an overview. Close-up lenses are for detailed photographs of evidence— such as fingerprints.

tripod A three-legged stand keeps the camera steady.

extra batteries For both the cameras and the flashes.

photo evidence rulers
Photographers place a ruler next to evidence before they take the picture. The ruler shows the real size of the evidence.

film Crime scene photographers need both color and black-and-white. Digital users need no film at all.

low-tech tools Blocks of wood and clothespins hold small evidence for close-ups. A white handkerchief can go over a flash to soften the light. A tape measure helps mark distances.

photograph markers
These numbers can be placed next to each piece of evidence. Later, in court, the evidence will be referred to by these numbers.

index cards and felt-tip pen
These are used to label evidence for mid-range and close-up photographs.

flashlight Keeps a photographer from stepping on important evidence in the dark.

notebooks and pens
These are used to make notes about photographs.

light meter
This gadget measures natural light. It tells photographers when a flash is needed.

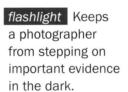

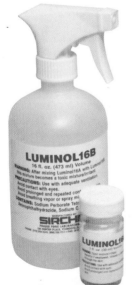

LUMINOL16B

luminol This chemical glows greenish blue when it comes in contact with blood. It is extremely sensitive and can detect even very faint traces of blood. Photographers use it to detect blood evidence at crime scenes.

Which is the REAL image?
It's nearly impossible to guess. But we'll give you a hint: The guy in the gray tank top has never met the other people in the photograph.

Digital Debate

Can computer photographs be trusted in court?

Have you ever played with a photo-editing program on the computer? It's not hard to cut and paste your sister's head onto Shrek's body. That's the power of digital photography.

Digital cameras capture images as computer files. Film photography captures pictures on film. Both film and digital images can be changed. But altering film takes many hours in a darkroom. You can change a digital image with a few clicks of a mouse.

As a result, crime scene photographers have stayed with film for a long time. Suppose a cop wanted a suspect to go free. Couldn't he simply alter an image of a fingerprint? It's possible. And that possibility could make judges and juries suspicious of digital photos.

DIGITAL IS HERE TO STAY

But courts are starting to accept digital photos as evidence. And many police departments are switching from film to digital. Digital photos are less expensive. Photographers can take more shots. They can also check what they're doing at the scene. "You only have one chance at a crime scene," says forensic technician Jaymie Spohn. "If you take a whole roll of blurry pictures, you won't know that until you develop the film. With digital, you can see if you are making a mistake and correct it right there."

The fact is, we live in a computer age. Film is probably on its way out. Digital is here to stay.

HELP WANTED: Crime Scene Photographer

Can you picture yourself as a crime scene photographer? Here's more information about this field.

24/7: How did you get interested in crime scene photography?

SPOHN: When I was in seventh grade, my mom had a book called *Fatal Vision*. It was about a famous true crime case. She let me read it, and it just fascinated me. But I never imagined I could get a job working with this kind of thing until I was in college.

Jaymie Spohn was a forensic technician in Fayetteville, NC. A big part of her job was crime scene photography.

24/7: What happened then?

SPOHN: I was majoring in biology. I wasn't sure what I wanted to do though. My advisor suggested forensics. It was like a gong went off in my head. I said, "That's it!" I graduated with a major in biology and two minors. One was in criminal justice. The other was chemistry.

24/7: What's a typical day like for a forensic technician?

SPOHN: My typical day started at night. I had the 11 P.M. to 8 A.M. shift. You could never tell what would happen. A few nights we didn't get a single call. Other nights we were going from scene to scene the whole time. You have to work

52

slowly and carefully on a crime scene. If you aren't finished when your shift is over, you have to keep working.

24/7: What was your favorite part of the job?

SPOHN: I loved that it was different every day. I loved the challenge of it.

24/7: What about cases where someone has died and you have to photograph the body?

SPOHN: Those are always very hard. But I was deeply moved by the victims and their families. I wanted to do my job as well as I possibly could for them. I wanted the person who had done the crime to be caught.

24/7: What's your advice to young people who are interested in forensic work?

SPOHN: Go for it! Make phone calls. Ask questions. Don't give up. And if you don't think it's in your nature to do crime scene work, consider lab work. It's less disturbing, but still really interesting.

THE STATS

MONEY
▶ Average yearly salary for a crime scene photographer in the U.S.: $35,000
▶ Average yearly salary for an experienced crime scene analyst: $55,000
▶ Average yearly salary for a supervisor of a crime scene photo lab: $70,000–$120,000

EDUCATION
▶ 4 years of college or 2 years with a major in criminal justice, science, or photography
▶ On-the-job training courses to learn about new technology

THE NUMBERS
▶ Number of people working in the Photography Unit of the Los Angeles Police Department (LAPD): 46
▶ Number of pictures the LAPD's Photography Unit printed in 2001: 1,062,336
▶ Number of requests for forensic services given to the 50 largest crime labs in the U.S. in 2002: 1.2 million

DO YOU HAVE WHAT IT TAKES?

Take this totally unscientific quiz to see if you have what it takes to be a crime scene photographer.

1 **Do you like taking photos?**
a) I love it. I'm the one snapping pics of all my friends.
b) Sure, it's fun sometimes.
c) No. I don't have a camera. I don't want one, either.

2 **When something bad happens, I...**
a) stay calm and try to figure out what to do next.
b) call my friend and complain about how bad it is.
c) panic and run away.

3 **Details are...**
a) exciting. I love to discover them.
b) interesting. Small things can be cool.
c) boring. Who has time for small stuff?

4 **Crime scene work can be pretty disturbing. I...**
a) have a stomach of iron. Nothing grosses me out.
b) don't like blood and guts, but I can take it.
c) get weak in the knees if I see blood.

5 **Technology is...**
a) really cool. I love learning the latest about computers and video.
b) OK. I can work with it when I need to.
c) not interesting at all to me. I try to avoid it.

YOUR SCORE

Give yourself 3 points for every "**a**" you chose. Give yourself 2 points for every "**b**" you chose. Give yourself 1 point for every "**c**" you chose.

If you got **13–15 points**, you'd probably be a good forensic photographer. If you got **10–12 points**, you might be a good forensic photographer. If you got **5–9 points**, you might want to look at another career!

HOW TO GET STARTED ... NOW!

It's not too early to start working toward your goals.

GET AN EDUCATION

▶ Starting now, take as many science and photography courses as you can. Train yourself to ask questions, gather evidence, and draw conclusions the way forensic scientists do.

▶ Start thinking about college. Look for ones that have criminal justice programs. Call or write to those colleges to get information. Here's a good place to start: **www.crime-scene-investigator.net/csi-training.html**

▶ Take pictures. Experiment with close-up, mid-range, and overview photos. Get to know how your camera really works. Experiment with lenses, focusing, and lighting.

▶ Read the newspaper. Keep up with what's going on in your community.

▶ Read anything you can find about crime scene photography. Check out books from the library on true crimes. See how investigators use crime scene photos. Mystery novels are good to read for fun, too. See the books and Web sites in the Resources section on pages 56–58.

▶ Graduate from high school!

NETWORK!

▶ Call your local law enforcement agency. Ask for the public affairs office. Find out if you can interview a crime scene photographer about his or her job.

GET AN INTERNSHIP

▶ Call the cops. Many police departments have programs for teen volunteers. You can get to know police work from the inside. You'll see if it's right for you.

LEARN ABOUT OTHER JOBS IN THE FIELD

▶ There are several jobs that include crime scene photography as one of their duties. They are:
**police officer
crime scene analyst
crime scene technician
forensic technician
detective
criminalist
crime lab supervisor**

55

Resources

Looking for more information about crime scene photography? Here are some resources you don't want to miss.

PROFESSIONAL ORGANIZATIONS

Evidence Photographers International Council, Inc. (EPIC)
www.epic-photo.org
600 Main Street
Honesdale, PA 18431
PHONE: 800-356-3742

EPIC is a nonprofit educational and scientific organization to promote the advancement of forensic photography and videography in civil evidence and law enforcement.

International Crime Scene Investigators Association (ICSIA)
www.icsia.org
PMB 385
15774 S. LaGrange Road
Orland Park, IL 60462
PHONE: 708-460-8082

The ICSIA was created to assist law enforcement personnel who are involved in the processing of crime scenes and to encourage the exchange of information related to crime scenes.

Law Enforcement and Emergency Services Video Association (LEVA)
www.leva.org
P.O. Box 126156
Fort Worth, TX 76126
PHONE: 817-249-1480

LEVA is a nonprofit organization committed to improving the quality of video training and promoting the use of state-of-the-art, effective equipment in the law enforcement and emergency services community.

In addition, many states have their own crime scene investigation organizations.

WEB SITES

Court TV's Crime Library
www.crimelibrary.com
This is a very big crime site with lots of information. Do searches on the site on topics like "Sam Sheppard" and "crime scene photography" to learn more.

Crime Scene and Evidence Photography
www.crime-scene-investigator.net/csi-photo.html
Provides links to articles by experts on crime scene and evidence photography, the role of digital photography, uses of infrared and ultraviolet photography, and more.

Crime Scene Photography
www.rcmp-learning.org/docs/ecdd1004.htm
Guidelines for crime scene photographers on how to approach the task of taking court-worthy forensic photographs.

The Fresh Eye
www.apogeephoto.com/mag3-6/mag3-7fresheye.shtml
Meet Martin Golden, a forensic photographer from Denver, Colorado, in this first-person article about crime scene photography as a career.

The Hole in the Wall Gang
www.geocities.com/cfpdlab/battery.html
More information on the Hole in the Wall Gang, including digital images of the battery that helped Detective Robert Kramer crack the case.

You Won't Believe Your Eyes
www.seanet.com/~rod/digiphot.html
This article offers background on the science of digital photography, and its plusses and problems in courtroom use.

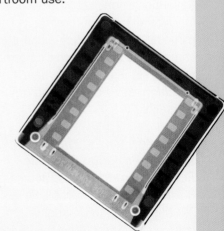

BOOKS

Camenson, Blythe. *Opportunities in Forensic Science Careers.* New York: McGraw-Hill, 2001. This book has information about training, education, salaries, and career opportunities in the field of forensics.

Evans, Colin. *The Casebook of Forensic Detection: How Science Solved 100 of the World's Most Baffling Crimes.* New York: Wiley, 1998. How fifteen different forensic techniques solved 100 celebrated cases from the 1700s through the 20th century.

Genge, Ngaire E. *The Forensic Casebook: The Science of Crime Scene Investigation.* New York: Ballantine Books, 2002. This book looks at all kinds of forensic crime-fighting, including a chapter on crime scene photography. It has exciting stories of real crimes. It also has information on jobs and training programs.

Rainis, Kenneth G. *Crime-Solving Science Projects: Forensic Science Experiments.* Berkeley Heights, N.J.: Enslow Publishing, 2000. Students learn about fingerprints, fibers, blood evidence, and other factors of forensic science.

Staggs, Steven. *Crime Scene and Evidence Photographer's Guide.* Wildomar: Calif.: Staggs Publishing, 1997. This handbook is carried around by many working crime scene photographers. It is also used as a textbook in college and police academy classes. It's a good overview of the technical side of crime scene photography.

Walker, Pam, and Elaine Wood. *Crime Scene Investigations: Real-Life Science Labs for Grades 6–12.* New York: Jossey-Bass, 1998. Find step-by-step experiments so kids can solve crimes just like real forensic scientists.

DVDS

The Best of Court TV: Body of Evidence (Story House Productions, 2002). A profile of Dayle Hinman, one of the nation's leading forensic scientists, and how she's cracked dozens of high-profile cases.

Cold Case Files— The Most Infamous Cases (A & E Home Video, 2005). Ten of the toughest true crimes and how they were solved.

Court TV—Forensic Files (Medstar Television, 2004). A series with detailed accounts of how notable crimes were solved with the help of forensic science.

A

analyze (AN-uh-lyz) *verb* to study a study a situation and figure it out

appeal (uh-PEEL) *verb* to ask a higher court to look at a legal decision and see if it was fair

B

biased (BYE-uhst) *adjective* prejudiced or favoring one point of view

C

close-up (KLOHSS-uhp) *adjective* or *noun* describes a photograph in which a small detail, like a fingerprint, fills up the whole picture (opposite of *overview*)

convicted (kuhn-VIK-tuhd) *adjective* proven guilty of a crime

coroner (KOR-uh-nur) *noun* someone who investigates suspicious deaths

crime scene photography (krime seen fuh-TOG-ruh-fee) *noun* the process of taking pictures of evidence after a crime happens

D

digital (DIJ-uh-tuhl) *adjective* describes a camera that records pictures on an electronic chip rather than on film. These pictures can be viewed right away but can also be easily changed on a computer.

E

evidence (EHV-uh-denss) *noun* things that prove that someone is innocent or guilty

expert (EX-purt) *noun* a person who knows a lot about a subject. See page 12 to learn more about forensic experts.

eyewitness (EYE-wit-nes) *noun* someone who saw a crime take place

F

FBI (EF-bee-eye) *noun* a U.S. government agency that investigates major crimes. It stands for *Federal Bureau of Investigation*.

filter (FILL-tur) *noun* a colored piece of plastic that goes over the lens of a camera

forensic photography (fuh-REN-sik fuh-TOG-ruh-fee) *noun* photography that can be used as evidence in the U.S. legal system

frame (fraym) *noun* what you see when you look through a camera to take a picture

I

investigator (in-VESS-tuh-gay-tuhr) *noun* someone who tries to figure out how a crime happened

J

juror (JUR-uhr) *noun* a person who serves on a jury. A jury is a group of people who listen to a court case and decide if someone is guilty or innocent.

L

latent prints (LATE-uhnt PRINTS) *noun* fingerprints that are not visible to the eye

lens (lenz) *noun* a curved piece of glass in a camera

luminol (LOO-min-ahl) *noun* a chemical that is sprayed on a surface to help detect blood

M

motive (MO-tihv) *noun* why someone does something

mid-range (mid-RAYNJ) *adjective* or *noun* describes a photograph that is between a close-up and an overview (see *close-up*, *overview*)

mug shot (mug shot) *noun* a photo taken of someone when he or she is charged with a crime

O

orphanage (OR-fuh-nij) *noun* a place where orphans—or children without parents—sometimes live

overview (OH-vuhr-vyoo) *adjective* or *noun* describes a photograph that captures the "big picture" of a crime scene (opposite of *close-up*)

P

photog (FUH-tog) *noun* short for *photographer*

photogrammetry (fo-tuh-GRAM-uh-tree) *noun* a scientific process for finding out the size of something by comparing it to other known measurements. This process can determine how tall a suspect caught on a security video is.

process (PRAH-sess) *verb* to gather evidence at a crime scene

prosecutor (prahs-uh-KYOO-tuhr) *noun* a person who tries to prove that the person on trial is guilty

S

staged (stajd) *adjective* describes a crime scene that a criminal changes to try to fool the police

suspect (SUS-pekt) *noun* a person who might be guilty of a crime

T

360 (three-SIKS-tee) *noun* an overview that captures all angles of a crime scene

V

valid (VAL-id) *adjective* legal; based on facts or evidence

visible (VIHZ-uh-bull) *adjective* describes what you can see

W

walkthrough (WAHLK-throo) *noun* the process of walking through a crime scene

wide-angle (WYD-ANG-gull) *adjective* describes a lens used in an overview photograph, which includes the largest and widest view of a subject

Index

Author's Note

The best part about doing my research for this book was talking to so many people who love their jobs! Crime scene photography attracts people who like technology and who are very curious. They solve problems creatively. And they have fun doing that. I also did research from books and from the Internet. But talking to people was definitely the most interesting part of my job.

I'd like to thank Jennifer DeSeo and Lisa Feder-Feitel for their research help on this book.

CONTENT ADVISER: King C. Brown, MS, CSCSA, CFPH, CLPE, Crime Scene Supervisor, West Palm Beach (Florida) Police Department